At Issue

| Distracted Driving

Other Books in the At Issue Series:

At Issue

I Distracted Driving

Stefan Kiesbye, Book Editor

GREENHAVEN PRESS
A part of Gale, Cengage Learning

GALE
CENGAGE Learning·

Detroit • New York • San Francisco • New Haven, Conn • Waterville, Maine • London

Elizabeth Des Chenes, *Managing Editor*

© 2012 Greenhaven Press, a part of Gale, Cengage Learning.

Gale and Greenhaven Press are registered trademarks used herein under license.

For more information, contact:
Greenhaven Press
27500 Drake Rd.
Farmington Hills, MI 48331-3535
Or you can visit our Internet site at gale.cengage.com

For product information and technology assistance, contact us at

Gale Customer Support, 1-800-877-4253
For permission to use material from this text or product, submit all requests online at www.cengage.com/permissions

Further permissions questions can be e-mailed to permissionrequest@cengage.com

Articles in Greenhaven Press anthologies are often edited for length to meet page requirements. In addition, original titles of these works are changed to clearly present the main thesis and to explicitly indicate the author's opinion. Every effort is made to ensure that Greenhaven Press accurately reflects the original intent of the authors. Every effort has been made to trace the owners of copyrighted material.

Cover image © Images.com/Corbis.

LIBRARY OF CONGRESS CATALOGING-IN-PUBLICATION DATA

Distracted driving / Stefan Kiesbye, book editor.
   p. cm. -- (At issue)
   Includes bibliographical references and index.
   ISBN 978-0-7377-5566-4 (hardcover) -- ISBN 978-0-7377-5567-1 (pbk.)
   1. Traffic safety--United States. 2. Automobile drivers--United States--Psychology. 3. Distraction (Psychology) I. Kiesbye, Stefan.
   HE5614.2.D57 2012
   363.12'51--dc23
                                                      2011035521

Printed in the United States of America
1 2 3 4 5 6 7 15 14 13 12

Contents

Introduction

To be sure, cell phones are not the only distractions on the road while driving. From eating hamburgers, yogurt, and even soup, to adjusting the car stereo, opportunities to take one's eyes off the road abound. However, cell phone use in cars has been on the rise for a number of years, and accidents caused by drivers who are texting or talking on phones while they are driving have increased. According to the September 23, 2010 issue of the *Christian Science Monitor*, "[t]exting while driving likely caused more than 16,000 road fatalities between 2002 and 2007." New legislation throughout the United States is attempting to ban texting-while-driving as well as the use of phones without hands-free devices. But increasing cell phone use, as well as other activities while driving, may just be symptoms of the actual cause for distracted driving—ever-increasing commutes.

"The United States has the highest rate of car ownership in the world, at 779 motor vehicles for every 1,000 man, woman and child," according to the Urban Bicycle Blog. "Americans on average sit in their cars for 48 minutes each day, and commuters in larger cities spend far more than this in their cars commuting to work."

One such case is that of Colin Deaso, a financial-service consultant who lives in Sterling, Virginia, but works in Washington DC. As reported by MSN.com's Lauren Barack in January 2008, "[h]e leaves the house at 6:30 a.m.; in the evening, he waits until he thinks traffic has cleared, getting home by about 7 p.m." Barack finds that for many Americans, "[s]acrificing hours each day on the road seems like a necessary trade-off . . . Many are willing to move farther away from their jobs as long as weekend time is spent in communities they like, where they can afford the kinds of homes they want." Differences in housing prices—often in the hundreds of thousands—might make that trade-off worthwhile at first, but the extra time spent away from home can be grating, or even feel like punishment. Nevertheless, many choose long commutes over smaller houses. A commuter who travels six hours daily to and from work admits to Barack, "When I first started I thought, 'I'm the only crazy person doing this' . . . But when I was walking to the parking lot . . . I noticed a lot of permit stickers on cars from my area. There were at least 60 or 70 people doing exactly the same thing."

Trying to utilize the time spent inside their cars, commuters engage in many different activities while driving, from listening to the radio to eating breakfast. Edmunds.com warns that, "you probably live out of your car as you shuttle between school, work and home. Your ride is your dressing room, your nightclub on wheels, your lunch room and even your meditation room. But, unfortunately . . . driving is a task that requires your undivided attention." However, as the time spent on the road increases—often in daily traffic jams and highway gridlock—the urge to do something other than stare at the bumper ahead becomes nearly irresistible. Articles directed at commuters recommend using time behind the wheel, offering such suggestions as listening to university lectures, recording brainstorms for business ideas on a digital recorder, or learning a foreign language. And while it's tempting to make use of what could otherwise be an unproductive drive, most commuters do not listen to lectures about Einstein's Theory of relativity but instead pick up their phones to chat or text.

Public transportation might increase commuter safety, but after the *New York Times* ran an article about European cities' initiatives to increase uses of rail and bus and curb car traffic, *Grist* reporter Sarah Goodyear noted that "[t]he comments section of the *Times* [was] loaded with people who protest that these European policies could never work in the US because we are such a big country. All that wide-open space, and stuff." In her article for *Grist*, Goodyear concludes that, "there are dozens, if not hundreds, of American cities that could easily incorporate more pedestrian- and transit-friendly policies. And yet even in New York City, with the lowest car ownership rates in the nation, it is a struggle to take a single inch away from cars."

In the meantime, the debate over cell phone use and distracted driving continues, while legislators look for new initiatives to help reduce accidents and fatalities. The articles selected for *At Issue: Distracted Driving* discuss various aspects of the problem, the challenges surrounding new laws banning texting-while-driving, as well as new technologies that might help make American roads safe.

1

Teens and Distracted Driving

Mary Madden and Amanda Lenhart

Mary Madden's research has covered the evolution of online music and video, the rise of social media, and teenagers' use of communication technologies. Amanda Lenhart directs the Pew Internet & American Life Project's research on teens, children, and families. She has also written about education, gaming, and networked communication tools like mobile phones, social networks, blogging, and microblogging.

Three quarters of American teenagers own a cell phone and two thirds of them send and receive text messages. In a 2009 survey conducted by the Pew Research Center's Internet and American Life Project, 800 teens (12-17) were questioned about their cell phone usage. A significant percentage noted that they have texted or talked while driving. Additionally, many of them talked about riding with distracted adult drivers who text, talk, and drive. Teenagers' acceptance of new technologies also leads to passive behavior when they encounter distracted driving among their friends and family. While many teenagers worry about cell phone use in cars, a majority of them accept risky behavior in themselves and others.

Over the summer of 2009, the Pew Research Center's Internet & American Life Project conducted a survey of 800 teens ages 12–17 asking about their experiences with cell phone use in cars: All of the teens in our survey were asked about their experiences as passengers, and if they were 16 or older and have a cell phone, they were also asked about their own actions behind the wheel. Additionally, the Project and the University of Michigan conducted 9 focus groups with teens ages 12–18 between June and October 2009 where the topic of driving and mobile phones was addressed.

Fully 75% of all American teens ages 12–17 now own a cell phone, and 66% use their phones to send or receive text messages. Older teens are more likely than younger teens to have cell phones and use text messaging; 82% of teens ages 16–17 have a cell phone and 76% text.

Overall, 34% of teen texters ages 16–17 say they have texted while driving. That translates into 26% of all American teens ages 16–17.

A Fast-growing Habit

Boys and girls are equally likely to report texting behind the wheel; 34% of each group say they have used text messaging while driving. At the same time, texting at the wheel is less common than having a conversation on the phone while driving. Looking at teens ages 16–17 who have a cell phone, 52% say they have talked on a cell phone while driving. That translates into 43% of all American teens ages 16–17.

Fully 75% of all American teens ages 12–17 now own a cell phone, and 66% use their phones to send or receive text messages.

However, it is important to note that some of these teens may use hands-free devices or a speakerphone function with their cell phones. This survey did not include questions to differentiate between conversations with handheld phones and those that took place with the assistance of a hands-free device or phone feature.

Indeed, in focus groups and written surveys conducted in partnership with the University of Michigan, some teens told us that they draw a line between conversations and texting, while others expressed concern over any activity that takes the driver's eyes off the road. One middle school-aged girl wrote: "I'm very concerned because to me it's not too safe to drive and text or talk (. . .) because you're looking down in order to read it or text back."

Likewise, one middle school-aged boy wrote: "I do worry about it because what if you're driving and not paying attention to the road you can hit someone or make them hit you."

One 9th–10th grade boy said, "People texting worries me more than people calling people, because texting is more distracting than talking on the phone because you can pay more attention to the road when talking than texting."

Socializing on the Road

The teens in our focus groups who said they texted while driving reported a variety of motivations for their behavior, including the need to report their whereabouts to friends and parents, getting directions and flirting with significant others. Teens also told of a variety of practices they use to try to increase safety while still maintaining the ability to text in the car. Some felt as though they could safely manage a quick exchange of texts while the car was stopped. One high school-aged boy shared that he would text "only at a stop sign or light but if it's a call they have to wait or I'll hand it to my brother or whoever is next to me."

Others told of holding the phone up to keep their eyes simultaneously on the road and the phone. "I try not to, but at a red light, it's a lot easier" said one high school boy. "And if I do text while I'm driving, I usually try to keep the phone up near the windshield, so if someone is braking in front of me or stops short, I'm not going to be looking down and hit them."

Some teens explained other methods for handling calls or texts while on the road "Most of my friends give me their phones to text for them and read their texts, so the driver doesn't do it themselves," wrote one older high school girl.

Ignoring the Dangers

Other teens were more blasé about texting in the car. Said one high-school aged boy: "I think it's fine . . . And I wear sunglasses so the cops don't see [my eyes looking down]." Likewise, another high school-aged girl wrote that she texts "all the time," and that "everybody texts while they drive (. . .) like when I'm driving by myself I'll call people or text them 'cause I get bored." One older high school-aged boy explained that he limits his texting while driving only if his parents are around: "I'm fine with it, just not with my mom and dad in the car. Like when I'm with my brother, I do it."

> *"People texting worries me more than people calling people, because texting is more distracting than talking on the phone because you can pay more attention to the road when talking than texting."*

Teens did make a distinction between reading text messages and sending them. "There's a difference, I think," said one older high school boy. "Because just reading a text isn't that bad, it's just reading and then moving on. If you're texting, it's going to take more time when you're supposed to be driving, and that's when most people get in accidents."

They also made a distinction between placing and answering calls on the phone in the car and sending and receiving text messages. "It's different because texting you mostly have to look down," said one middle school boy. "[While] calling you're still mostly focused but you could get into conversations and not be aware of what's going on and stuff." Another high school boy wrote: "It depends on what the driver is doing—texting or calling. If he's texting, to me that's a dangerous thing. If the driver is using the phone to chat with people, I am worried, but if he or she uses the phone [in] an emergency, I'm not worried as much."

Distracted Drivers with Teens as Passengers

Among all teens ages 12–17, 48% say they have been in a car when the driver was texting. The older teens in our sample reported a higher incidence of this experience; while 32% of teens ages 12–13 say they have been passengers in a car while the driver was texting at the wheel, 55% of those ages 14–17 report this. Looking only at those who are of driving age—16 and 17 year-olds—the rate jumps to 64%.

In a separate question, teens ages 12–17 were asked if they had been in a car when the driver used the cell phone in a way that put themselves or others in danger. Four in ten teens (40%) said they had been in a risky situation like this. Younger teens ages 12–13 are generally less likely to say they have been in a car with a driver who used a cell phone in a dangerous way; 34% report this, compared with 42% of those ages 14–17. Teens of driving age (16–17) are the most likely to report this experience; 48% have been a passenger in a car with a driver who used a cell phone in a risky way.

However, it is important to note that the survey question wording does not identify the age of the distracted driver. The teens who were interviewed in the phone survey could be reporting experiences as passengers with adult drivers or other teen drivers. Indeed, as noted above, in the focus group setting, many teens relayed accounts of their parents or other adult relatives texting and talking while driving. While this was cause for concern for some, others felt that their parents and others were "good drivers" who could manage their phones safely.

Texting in the Car

When asked whether he had any concerns about safety when a driver uses the phone, one middle school-aged boy wrote: "I am concerned because when my mom drives she talks on the phone a lot so she is still alert but she can get kind of dangerous." Another 9th/10th grade boy said "Yeah [my dad] he drives like he's drunk. His phone is just like sitting right in front of his face, and he puts his knees on the bottom of the steering wheel and tries to text."

The frequency of teens reporting parent cell phone use behind the wheel in our focus groups was striking, and suggested that, in many cases, texting while driving is a family affair. When one middle school-aged boy was asked how often he was in a moving vehicle when the driver sends a text message, he replied: "All the time. My mom, sister or brother will sit behind the wheel the whole time and just text away." Similarly, a middle school girl told us: "My uncle will drive and text while he is driving—he will text no matter where he is."

Other teen respondents referred to their parents' use of the phone while driving as part of a larger societal norm. One middle school-aged girl wrote: "I don't really get worried because everyone does it. And when my mother is texting and driving I don't really make a big deal because we joke around with her about it (cuz she's a crazy driver) but we don't take it so serious."

"I am concerned because when my mom drives she talks on the phone a lot so she is still alert but she can get kind of dangerous."

Texting was not the only cause for concern among the teens who participated in our focus groups. We also heard about the distractions of drivers trying to access Global Positioning System (GPS) information while cars were in motion. And some teens cited other applications available on smartphones that take the driver's eyes off the road. "My dad, he wasn't really texting, but when he drives, he has a GPS on his Blackberry, so when he's driving, he looks down at his phone" said one middle school boy, ". . . so it's like the same [as] being distracted from the road. My mom always gets on him about how it's unsafe and stuff."

Fully 73% of texting teens ages 16–17 have been in a car when the driver was texting. Half (52%) say they have been in a car when the driver used a cell phone in a dangerous way.

However, many of the teens we spoke with relayed experiences as passengers being driven by other young drivers. One young high school girl wrote about how often she's a passenger with drivers who text: "Every time I leave to go somewhere with my brother or sister and my friends. Every time!" Another high school age girl wrote: "My sister does it despite my mother's warnings, so does my brother and my friends despite my warnings."

Teen Texters Are More Likely Passengers of a Distracted Driver

Teens ages 12–17 who use text messaging report a higher incidence of being passengers when the driver is texting or otherwise using the cell phone in a dangerous way. Among all teen texters, 58% say they have been in a car while the driver was texting. That compares with just 28% of non-texting teens. Similarly, 44% of texting teens say they have been in a car when the driver was using a cell phone in a way that put themselves or others in danger, while 31% of non-texting teens have had this experience.

Older texting teens ages 16–17 are even more likely to be in the company of drivers who use their cell phones while at the wheel. Fully 73% of texting teens ages 16–17 have been in a car when the driver was texting. Half (52%) say they have been in a car when the driver used a cell phone in a dangerous way.

Teens in our focus groups had a variety of responses to these situations—some were adamant and angry about being endangered. One high school boy was asked about riding with drivers who text: "Not if they know what's good for them. I'll snatch the phone out of your hands—don't be driving in the car with me and doing that . . . I want to live until the end of this car ride."

Others were less concerned: "It doesn't really bother me," wrote one high school boy, "I've made and received calls almost every time I've driven." Another high school boy wrote: "I worry about if they can do it. If they know what they're doing and looking up every second. I usually watch the road when it happens and tell them if they're going off the road or something. I don't really care though."

2

Efforts to Curb Distracted Driving May Be Misguided

Jayne O'Donnell

Jayne O'Donnell is a consumer reporter covering retail, fraud, and auto and product safety at USA Today. *She has won several public service and journalism awards for her work alerting the public to auto safety hazards, and is the author of* Gen BuY: How Tweens, Teens and Twenty-Somethings Are Revolutionizing Retail.

While cell phone use is undoubtedly a major distraction for drivers, the government's focus on banning hand-held devices and texting is misguided. There are many different distractions while driving and available data is sketchy at best when it comes to determining which distraction is responsible for a given accident. Furthermore, the auto industry's desire to provide consumers with new and flashy gadgets that require drivers to take their eyes off the road undermines any legislative initiatives.

Transportation Secretary Ray LaHood regularly refers to distracted driving as an "epidemic." Toyota said last week [January 2011] it will spend $50 million on research into issues including distracted driving, a "growing cause of accidents." And state legislators are racing to enact laws banning what they see as the culprit: text messaging and handheld cellphones.

Yet the Insurance Institute for Highway Safety [IIHS] says there's no evidence that distracted driving is leading to more crashes or that laws banning texting or handheld cells are having any effect, possibly because hands-free phones can be just as dangerous.

Distracted driving "is a growing problem in the sense of our recognition of it, but the fact is, it's always been there," says Adrian Lund, president of IIHS, which has worked with the Transportation Department's National Highway Traffic Safety Administration [NHTSA] for years.

No one is suggesting distracted driving isn't a safety issue or that texting or talking on a phone would improve anyone's driving. And, as Governors Highway Safety Association [GHSA] Executive Director Barbara Harsha notes, a "public outcry" against cellphone use while driving has motivated federal and state officials to act.

Many safety experts question such a high-profile national campaign on the issue when there is so little reliable data on how distraction is contributing to crashes—and so much data on how to prevent deaths and injuries from other causes. Some are unwilling to speak publicly against LaHood, who has lashed out repeatedly at IIHS over its "misleading" cellphone research.

No one is suggesting distracted driving isn't a safety issue or that texting or talking on a phone would improve anyone's driving.

Transportation Department officials say they are not ignoring other safety issues at the expense of distracted driving and cite recent safety standards, including one requiring better rear visibility in vehicles to prevent back-over deaths; a new five-star car-rating system; and a record number of recalls.

In a statement, LaHood said the department has been "laser focused on auto safety, holding automakers accountable for dangerous safety defects that put consumers at risk. . . .

Our roads are the safest they've ever been, but we're not going to stop pressing forward to make them safer."

A Bias in the Data

LaHood's distracted-driving focus dates to soon after *The New York Times* reported in July 2009 that NHTSA covered up a report calling hands-free cellphones even riskier than hand-held ones. At about the same time, a teenage girl near his hometown in Illinois was killed, purportedly while texting. The hands-free-phone report was released after a Freedom of Information Act request, but DOT [Department of Transportation] maintains it is "flawed." It is working on new research expected to be published next year.

Thursday, LaHood will join safety advocates and businesses to celebrate the one-year anniversary of FocusDriven, a new advocacy group described as being like MADD, which is aimed at drunken drivers, to combat distracted driving.

The DOT says distracted driving was linked to 10% of fatal crashes in 2005. That increased to 16% in 2008 and leveled off at 16% in 2009, thanks to DOT's efforts.

Although studies by IIHS and others show using a cellphone while driving quadruples the risk of a crash, IIHS research shows there was no concurrent increase in crashes as the number of cellphones increased throughout the 2000s. The institute is also studying how states "code" crash causes from police reports. Lund says it could be that changes in the numbers are due to more concern about distracted driving, rather than more distracted-driving crashes.

"That's a bias in the data," he says, noting IIHS is "wary" of using it to measure distracted driving over time.

Many people involved in a crash or stopped by a police officer for bad driving wouldn't acknowledge cellphone use to a police officer because they'd fear getting cited for reckless driving, says Harsha. She calls it a "really, really challenging issue to collect data on and . . . to enforce the laws."

A New Flood of Distractions

In an analysis of 7,000 crashes released in September, NHTSA concluded 30% involved some type of distraction but found that of 14 sources of distraction in a car, texting while driving was the only one that was not a factor. (The Transportation Department notes it studied crashes in 2005 through 2007 and the number of monthly text messages has increased from about 7 billion in 2005 to about 173 billion in 2010.)

Driving while talking on, dialing or hanging up a phone was linked to 3.4% of the crashes, looking at other objects in the car was associated with 3.2% and talking with a passenger was a factor in nearly 16% of crashes, the largest percentage.

Cellphones are "yet another thing that's distracting people," but a "flood of new distractions are being built into vehicles," says Flaura Winston, scientific director at the Center for Injury Research and Prevention at The Children's Hospital of Philadelphia. Laws banning texting or handheld phones are "not the panacea," as drivers will find something else to distract them, she says.

The DOT [Department of Transportation] says distracted driving was linked to 10% of fatal crashes in 2005. That increased to 16% in 2008 and leveled off at 16% in 2009, thanks to DOT's efforts.

Automakers, which are regulated by NHTSA, are actively supporting LaHood's effort on distracted driving. They almost uniformly support bans on handheld cellphones but would oppose efforts to restrict hands-free calls. Mike Stanton, CEO of the Association of International Automobile Manufacturers, says his group's priority for state legislation will be getting texting and handheld bans passed that apply to all drivers and allow police to pull over people just for using their phones while driving. Stanton says there is not enough research to support restrictions on hands-free phones.

Carmakers have an interest in preserving drivers' ability to talk on the phone, at least with a headset or speakerphone, as many vehicles have phone-related technology.

Kids are Dying and Getting Hurt

Winston says she is "thrilled that we have a secretary of Transportation who's out there talking about crash-injury protection (and) really raising the consciousness that injuries and crashes are preventable." But she wishes legislatures would focus on "the bread-and-butter injury-protection policies that we know work," including laws about seat belts and booster seats.

"The challenge is they're not the hot issue right now," says Winston, a pediatrician and professor.

States, which need approval from NHTSA on how they spend federal dollars, have also been reducing the money spent on child-passenger protection in favor of distracted and impaired driving, says child-safety advocate Joseph Colella of Traffic Safety Projects.

Carmakers have an interest in preserving drivers' ability to talk on the phone, at least with a headset or speakerphone, as many vehicles have phone-related technology.

In September, NHTSA reported deaths to children under 14 were down 3% in 2009, but Colella says the agency failed to mention that deaths to children 1 through 6 were up 18% that year. That, he says, shows it's important to focus on protecting adults and children with belts and child seats in the crashes that do occur.

"Decisions are being made on incomplete info, and kids are dying and getting hurt," says Colella. DOT says the number of child deaths is down sharply from a few years ago, and the small numbers—503 children through age 7 were killed in 2009—can lead to big fluctuations each year.

GHSA's Harsha says the group has "mixed feelings" about states' focus on cellphones over issues such as tougher seat belt laws. But, "Getting legislatures to pay attention to any highway safety issue is probably better than them not paying attention at all."

"Is it the right priority? That remains to be seen," says Harsha. "But sometimes you just have to go where the opportunity presents itself."

3

Efforts to Ban Cell Phone Use While Driving Are Misguided

Andrew Ferguson

Andrew Ferguson, a senior editor at the Weekly Standard, *is the author of* Crazy U: One Dad's Crash Course in Getting His Kid Into College. *His columns have been published in* Fortune *and* TV Guide, *and he has written for the* New Yorker, *the* Los Angeles Times, *and the* New York Times.

Ignoring available studies and statistics, the government is not focusing on the many facets of distracted driving but solely on texting bans and laws prohibiting the use of hand-held phones in cars. Trying to look decisive, Secretary of Transportation Ray LaHood is overstating his case, creating frenzy and panic instead of approaching the problem systematically and effectively.

If you want to know why it may soon be illegal for you to use your cell phone when you drive your car, you have to remember that Ray LaHood, the secretary of transportation, is a government guy. It's all he knows.

As a young man LaHood taught for six years in a private school, but since then it's been government all the way—a few years as a planner for the state planning commission, a term in the Illinois legislature, nearly 20 years as a congressional aide, and 14 years in the big time, as a Republican congressman piping federal grants into a derelict district in central Illinois. Though he's driven many automobiles and ridden in countless airplanes, he has no particular expertise in the nation's transportation systems, and some kibitzers wondered aloud why President [Barack] Obama appointed him secretary. But the kibitzers miss the point: As a government guy LaHood doesn't need any expertise beyond being a government guy.

Campaigning Against Distracted Driving

This is where you and your cell phone come in. Over the last several months LaHood has mobilized his vast and lavishly funded ($70 billion) department behind a high-minded goal: "to put an end to distracted driving." Those are his words— not *curtail*, not *discourage*, not even *reduce* by 50 percent. No: *Put an end to.* In its ambition and method, LaHood's initiative is a kind of textbook example of how government guys create work for themselves, manage to keep themselves busy, and put the rest of us on our guard.

The government guy's first step, always, is to raid the language of epidemiology and declare a problem—any problem, from anorexia to obesity—an "epidemic." And so: "Distracted driving is a serious, life-threatening epidemic," LaHood said at one of his big events last month. (By definition, of course, epidemics are serious and life-threatening, but since distracted driving isn't really an epidemic, the adjectives are needed to juice it up.)

Even imaginary epidemics need victims. The next step is for the government guy to identify dead people whose relatives are willing, for unknown reasons, to let him publicly exploit their unutterable grief for his own purposes. To advance his distracted driving campaign LaHood keeps several of these abject relatives handy, so his publicists can position them just behind him and slightly to the right, where the cameras catch them gazing at him with liquid, upcast eyes. The relatives are particularly useful if some cynic or pantywaist naysayer questions the urgency or logic of a government initiative. When his use of statistics was called into question a few weeks ago, LaHood fired back on his website. "Ask Shelli Ralls," he said, "who lost her son Chance Wayne Wilcox on March 22, 2008" in a "crash caused by a cell phone driver." Here he inserted a tasteful picture of Wilcox's crash site. And then he invoked the deity. "Ask any one of the hundreds of people who have poured out their stories of loss on *Oprah*." Nothing shuts up a cynic like a grieving mother.

The government guy's first step, always, is to raid the language of epidemiology and declare a problem—any problem, from anorexia to obesity—an "epidemic."

Epidemic isn't the only essential term for a government guy. Certain phrases act as a kind of dog whistle for bureaucrats, activists, and sympathetic reporters, to let them know an important initiative is afoot. In seeking to end distracted driving in the United States, LaHood has used them all. He has issued a "call to action," vowed to "raise awareness," invoked a "national network" of "stakeholders" pursuing "best practices," insisted that "the American people" "demand action" and "commonsense solutions."

The Definition of Distracted Driving

The most valuable term for LaHood is "distracted driving." It is an expansive phrase that a deft government guy can play like an accordion, stretching or squeezing it as his argument demands. The immediate upshot of LaHood's initiative, he said last month [January, 2010], is that he wants laws that will make it illegal for drivers to use handheld cell phones behind the wheel. State laws, local laws, federal laws, whichever, it seems not to matter to him—just so long as this little slice of unregulated human behavior is prohibited and punished. Already seven states and the District of Columbia have outlawed the use of handheld cell phones by drivers, and dozens more are entertaining similar legislation. LaHood urges Congress to push all states to pass cell phone laws or, if the states fail him, to pass a law of its own.

It's a big step, telling people that they can't hold a cell phone in their car, but the fuzzy phrase "distracted driving" makes it look smaller, more reasonable, and much less intrusive than it is. Department of Transportation literature defines distracted driving as "any non-driving activity a person engages in that has the potential to distract him or her from the primary task of driving and increase the risk of crashing." Elsewhere the department offers a partial list of those dangerous nondriving activities in addition to holding a cell phone: "eating, drinking, conversing with passengers, interaction with in-vehicle technologies [I think this means changing the radio station], daydreaming, or dealing with strong emotions," along with other activities unspecified.

The fatality statistic doesn't tell us anything about cell phone use because it doesn't mention cell phone use.

Quite a list! But LaHood doesn't mention it when he appears at events designed to "raise awareness" about the dangers of handheld cell phone use. At a typical event last month [January, 2010] he announced that "nearly 6,000 people died in 2008 in crashes involving a distracted or inattentive driver," with the implication that a cell phone driving ban would halt the butchery—I mean epidemic.

Data Is Inconclusive

The real-world situation, you won't be surprised to learn, is more complicated. The precise number of these fatalities in 2008 was 5,870. According to the official tables, they occurred in "police-reported crashes in which at least one form of distracted driving was reported on the crash report." The fatality statistic doesn't tell us anything about cell phone use because it doesn't mention cell phone use. It doesn't even tell us whether "distracted driving," in any of its dozen or more manifestations, was the cause of the fatal crash. An Alzheimer's sufferer who got hit by a dump truck while driving through an oil slick and taking blows from his angry wife with the family dog perched on his shoulder sticking its disgusting tongue in his ear would become, in LaHood's statistical accounting, another piece of evidence for a ban on cell phone driving.

So what do we know about the safety of using cell phones in cars? Aside from the intuitive understanding that we all share—that anyone who can't wait till he's done driving to talk on his cell phone is a jackass—we don't know a lot for certain. The number of fatal crashes "involving distraction" has increased in the last four years; but the overall number of such crashes has declined. Nationwide, car crashes have fallen dramatically while the use of cell phones has jumped dramatically (from 195 billion minutes in June 2000 to 1.1 trillion in June 2008). Last month [January, 2010] the Highway Loss Data Institute issued a report comparing collision rates for states before and after they passed bans on drivers using handheld cell phones. The bans showed no effect on the number, frequency, or severity of collisions.

The number of fatal crashes "involving distraction" has increased in the last four years; but the overall number of such crashes has declined.

LaHood's reaction to this latest report showed why he's the government guy. It should have been a devastating blow; the institute's evidence severely undercuts the logic of his initiative. Instead he took to his blog—yes, even Ray LaHood has a blog—and summarily declared that the new study provided still more evidence that government action was urgently needed.

"The surprising data," he wrote, "encourages people to wrongly conclude that talking on cell phones while driving is not dangerous! Nothing could be further from the truth. Just ask Jennifer Smith . . ." Smith, of course, is another grieving mother. He went on to equate cell phone driving with drunk driving. "If anything, the study suggests we need even tougher protections."

Interpreting Statistics

How so? LaHood had an explanation for why the state bans had not reduced collisions. In states that banned handheld cell phone use, he said, drivers probably began using hands free cell phones. And "research tells us hands free is just as dangerous as handheld."

Thus the call to action escalates, and the needed prohibitions grow more comprehensive. A ban on handheld cell phone use will be insufficient if we are to cure the epidemic. Only a total ban on drivers' use of cell phones, handheld and hands-free, will bring progress.

LaHood didn't go further, at least for the moment. He might have mentioned that "research" also tells us that talking on a cell phone, hands free or handheld, is just as "dangerous" as having a spirited conversation with a passenger, which can be just as dangerous as drunk driving . . . and so on through the official list of distractions: eating, drinking, daydreaming . . .

We are, in other words, going to need a very big ban, and Ray LaHood is just the guy to give it to us. "Studies of cognitive distraction," he wrote on his blog, "tell us that it's not about where your hands are, but where your head is." It is a dream almost too big even for the most ambitious government guy: a National Initiative for Head Relocation.

4

Texting While Driving Is as Dangerous as Drunk Driving

Stephanie Hanes

Stephanie Hanes is a journalist whose work has appeared in more than a dozen national publications, including Smithsonian *magazine, the* Christian Science Monitor, Africa Geographic, *and* USA Today. *For several years, she covered southern Africa and related topics. She is writing a book about Gorongosa and American aid in Africa.*

While there are many distractions for drivers, cell phone use— especially texting—has become the main target of police and lawmakers. But legislation intended to fight traffic fatalities is hard to enforce, and new studies show that drivers are addicted to using their phones, decreasing chances of successful consumer education. Since many drivers overestimate their ability to multitask behind the wheel and put themselves and others at risk, scientists are working on devices that would make it impossible to receive calls in a moving vehicle, and new technologies might have a hand in curbing dangerous texting-while-driving habits.

Jennifer Smith, a Texas real estate agent, remembers when she considered her car an office, her cellphone a professional lifeline. If it rang, she picked it up. If she thought of information to share, she dialed. She knew that it wasn't the best idea to chat while driving, of course, but it wasn't illegal, and she didn't want to lose clients. Besides, she figured, she was careful.

But then, in September last year [2008], a driver using a cellphone plowed through a red light and slammed into Ms. Smith's mother's mini-SUV. Linda Doyle, who'd been on her way to pick up cat food for the Central Oklahoma Humane Society, where she was a regular volunteer, died the next morning.

"He is you and I. He is not just a teenager who doesn't care. I didn't understand how someone like that could just drive through a light without seeing it."

A Deadly Epidemic

During the excruciating months that followed, Smith couldn't shake the feeling that something about the crash didn't make sense. The driver who killed her mother was a sober, church going 20-year-old who'd never even had a speeding ticket. He had been on the phone for less than a minute. Visibility on the road was excellent. But the police report said that when a trooper asked him what color the traffic light had been, the distraught young man responded that he never saw it. He'd crashed into the driver's side of Ms. Doyle's car at nearly 50 m.p.h.; there weren't even skid marks at the scene.

"He's a good kid," Smith says. "He is you and I. He is not just a teenager who doesn't care. I didn't understand how someone like that could just drive through a light without seeing it. So I started researching."

The more she found, the angrier she became. Study upon study showed that talking on a cellphone while driving was far more dangerous than she'd realized—that a driver on a phone had the same reaction speed as someone legally intoxicated, that those talking on a phone behind the wheel are four times as likely to crash, that texting while driving is even more dangerous. And studies repeatedly showed that hands-free headsets—sometimes advertised as safer—were no less dangerous.

"I was just astonished," she says. Soon, Smith joined a growing movement of crash victims' families, academic researchers, and public-safety advocates campaigning against "distracted driving."

Fighting to Change Driving Laws

This public-safety movement has for years lobbied state legislatures to change driving laws, worked with schools and student groups, and pressured the federal government and industries to set new cellphone regulations. But momentum has picked up recently with some high-profile fatal crashes, including a number involving teens texting while driving. And last month, in what many saw as a coming of age for the movement, the US Department of Transportation hosted a distracted driving summit, where Secretary of Transportation Ray LaHood called for action against what he termed a "deadly epidemic."

"Distracted driving is a menace to society. And it seems to be getting worse every year," he said.

But he and others say that the fight against distracted driving could be much harder than other public-safety efforts, including the anti-drunken-driving movement that swept the country in the 1980s.

Far more people talk on their cellphones and use other electronic gadgets in the car than drive drunk, safety officials say. A generation of text-happy teenagers are getting their driver's licenses, and established drivers are increasingly buying smart phones that allow for distracting activity beyond just texting and talking—GPS [global positioning satellite] and entertainment devices, too, pull eyes and mental focus off the road.

And even where hand-held phone use in cars is banned—as it is in California, Connecticut, New Jersey, New York, Oregon, Washington, the District of Columbia, and the Virgin Islands—enforcement is difficult. One study observing New

York drivers, for instance, showed that the law did little to reduce the number of drivers with phones to ears.

While dozens of countries—from Australia to Zimbabwe—take a harsh view of this behavior and have banned hand-held phones in cars, there is little social stigma in the US.

Moreover, some research suggests that Americans are actually addicted to their phones. Harvard University psychiatrist John Ratey and other researchers have found that the brain receives a rush when it processes a text message or ring—the same high a gambler feels when hitting the jackpot.

[R]esearchers have found that the brain receives a rush when it processes a text message or ring—the same high a gambler feels when hitting the jackpot.

Battling Cell Phone Addiction

"It is a complex problem," says David Strayer, who studies cellphones and driving at the University of Utah. "We may have gotten ourselves into an addiction that we might not be able to get out of."

'Distracted Driving' is a catchall term that can include all sorts of behavior behind the wheel, from eating to applying makeup to texting. A distracted driver has what psychologists call "inattention blindness"—the brain does not process what is physically within eyesight, such as a red light.

The movement against distracted driving has increasingly focused on what it considers a deadly mix of two American passions: the automobile and new technology.

"There are always going to be distractions," says David Teater, senior director of transportation strategic initiatives at the National Safety Council, whose 12-year-old son was killed in a crash caused by a driver on a cellphone. "But the advent of mobile electronic communication devices has really changed the game because they've become so phenomenally prolific in such a short period of time. We've been talking on the phone for 80 years. We've been driving 100 years. It's only recently that we've tried to combine the two."

Most drivers say they're not happy about sharing the road with others trying the new technology.

A 2009 AAA [Automobile Association of America] Foundation study found that 91.5 percent of drivers considered talking on the phone while driving a serious threat to their safety; 97 percent said it was completely unacceptable to send a text or e-mail while driving. But two-thirds of those people admitted talking on their own phones while driving, and 1 in 7 have texted while driving.

A Pervasive Habit

Similarly, a National Highway Traffic Safety Administration study, in which data collectors observed drivers, estimated that 6 percent of drivers at any time are on the phone.

At the University of Utah's Applied Cognition Laboratory, Professor Strayer has been testing this do-as-I-say theory for a decade. Using neuroimaging and a drive simulator, he and his colleagues have watched what happens when drivers—including those who claim to be able to text, tweet, and talk safely at the wheel—mix cellphones and cars.

Unlike a conversation with a passenger sharing the same physical space of the car, the electronic conversation takes a driver into a virtual space away from the road.

The results are stark: Almost nobody multiprocesses the way they think they can. For 98 percent of the population, regardless of age, the likelihood of a crash while on a cellphone increases fourfold; the reaction to simulated traffic lights, pedestrians, and vehicles is comparable to that of someone legally intoxicated.

Although some critics claim that the simulator isn't real enough, studies of real-life driving in Canada and Australia had similar findings.

Strayer also found little difference between those using hand-held cellphones and those on hands-free headsets. The disruption, he says, is cognitive. Unlike a conversation with a passenger sharing the same physical space of the car, the electronic conversation takes a driver into a virtual space away from the road.

"We record brain activity," Strayer says, "and we can show that it's, suppressed from the cellphone conversation."

Interpreting the Data About Crashes

But where, cellphone proponents ask, are the crashes? While the number of cellphone subscribers has rocketed to 270 million in the US—the number of auto fatalities has remained stable, at about 40,000 deaths a year. The US Department of Transportation estimates that 6,000 of those are the result of distracted driving, but it has no specific statistics for phone-related deaths. The number of crashes has also remained steady.

"There have been some suggestions by researchers that the risk [of crash] is increased exponentially due to talking on the cellphone," says John Walls, spokesman for CTIA-The Wireless Association, which represents the cellphone industry. "Yet, for whatever reason, we haven't seen that play out in the number of accidents that occur. Although I would never suggest that that means to talk more in the car."

He says that his group does not take a stance on phoning-while-driving legislation.

"This is one of the key questions we're trying to unravel," says Russ Rader, spokesman for the Insurance Institute for Highway Safety. Mr. Rader says his group is studying how much the fatality rate should have dropped, given increased safety measures—such as better road construction and improved braking systems—as a way to gauge the real impact of cellphone use.

While the number of cellphone subscribers has rocketed to 270 million in the US—the number of auto fatalities has remained stable, at about 40,000 deaths a year.

Another explanation for the statistics, safety experts say, is that people tend to lie about their phone use in crashes. And without a subpoena for cellphone records, there's no way to check. There's often no box on the police report to check if the driver admits cellphone use.

An Uphill Battle

The lack of solid statistics means that advocates are constantly explaining themselves and often face an uphill battle in convincing legislatures to enact new cellphone laws.

But recently, the legislative tide has started to turn—thanks, in large part, to text messaging.

Texting drivers are easy to spot. Like drunken drivers, they're the ones going too slow or too fast, or weaving, says Gregory Massak, the police chief of Shirley, Mass. "They're concentrating more on [the phone] than on driving."

His officers are well aware of the impact of this behavior. In September [2009], an 18-year-old died when she crashed her car into a tree seconds after receiving a text message.

But Chief Massak says he has never issued a ticket for texting. In Massachusetts, he explains, there are no laws against cellphones in cars.

This may well change. Swayed in part by a number of highly publicized texting-while-driving deaths, 18 states and the District of Columbia have passed laws banning texting while driving; nine additional states prohibit teenagers from texting behind the wheel. This summer [2009], Sen. Charles

Schumer of New York introduced legislation that would withhold 25 percent of federal highway funding to states that don't institute some sort of texting ban. And last month [October, 2009], President Obama signed an executive order banning federal employees from sending texts in government cars.

Texting is a "perfect storm" of distraction, with cognitive, manual, and visual elements, says Strayer. "And it's primarily teenagers who are doing it. To become a proficient driver takes a few years, so it's the worst combination—a novice driver multitasking in a way [that takes] their eyes off the road."

"I prefer to text and drive rather than talk and drive. I can put the phone down in the middle of the text if something is going on."

For Teenagers, Texting Is Second Nature

To those who don't text regularly, these dangers might seem obvious. But for many teens, and a growing number of adults, texting is a central way of communicating—a virtual conversation that doesn't stop in the car. Even with the growing restrictions, 73 percent of teens admit to texting while driving, according to a Students Against Destructive Decisions (SADD) study.

"Some of them say that they're good at typing without looking at the screen; others say they hold it up by their eyes as they text," says Stephen Wallace, national chairman and CEO of SADD.

Heather Barrett, a college student in Ohio, says she probably receives and sends more than 500 messages a day: "I prefer to text and drive rather than talk and drive. I can put the phone down in the middle of the text if something is going on."

She says that she has caught herself swerving while texting—"but only on backcountry lanes, and never in traffic."

Joshua Weller, a scientist with Decision Research, has studied the perception of risk associated with distracted driving. His preliminary findings suggest a multilayered understanding of risk, similar to the way someone might internalize warnings against smoking. Those with a deeper appreciation of the risks of texting or talking on the phone—people who understand, for instance, that texting while driving 55 m.p.h. is similar to driving the length of a football field with one's eyes closed—are less likely to do it.

But establishing a widespread social understanding of risk is difficult. So is enforcement. It's hard to catch a texting driver, and it's too early to know the impact of texting laws.

Some safety advocates, then, are placing hope in technology to fight technology. Mr. Teater says there are systems in development that block incoming texts when a phone is in a car, responding with an automatic, "Sorry, I'm driving" message.

"We've got to rush technology to the market," he says. "There are a lot of people who will choose to not use phones while driving if there's a way not to do it but also stay in touch with people. We're going to have a nightmare on our hands if we don't get ahead of it."

5

Laws Against Texting While Driving Are Ineffective

Ashley Halsey, III

Ashley Halsey, III is a staff writer for the Washington Post, *frequently writing on traffic and transportation issues.*

Despite the current epidemic of texting while driving, fatal crashes in the United States have not spiked, and even though many state legislators get tough on distracted drivers, new laws have failed to make an impact. At best, cell phone bans around the country might take years to become effective, just like drunk driving laws before them; at worst they may prove as futile as anti-speeding campaigns of the past.

It's been almost 150 years since the first speeding law took effect, yet people speed all the time, and even strict enforcement has limited impact.

Text messaging has been around for about a dozen years, with public surveys showing overwhelming agreement that it's a dangerous distraction while driving. And laws against it have had little effect, according to a new study issued Tuesday [September 28, 2010].

New Laws Might Be Ineffective

The report by the Highway Loss Data Institute, an insurance industry-funded research group, compared crash rates in four states that prohibit texting with those in states where it is allowed. It found no reduction in states where it is banned.

"The point of texting bans is to reduce crashes, and by this essential measure the laws are ineffective," said Adrian Lund, president of the research group and of the affiliated Insurance Institute for Highway Safety.

An estimated 450,000 people were killed or injured last year in distracted-driving accidents.

Text messaging has been around for about a dozen years, with public surveys showing overwhelming agreement that it's a dangerous distraction while driving.

Lund says that while state legislatures are increasing speed limits to 75 mph [miles per hour], safety efforts have been "sidetracked" by a focus on reports of unintended acceleration and distracted driving.

"The hyper-visibility of these issues diverts attention from initiatives that have far greater potential to save lives," Lund said in August [2010]. "We need to look for the next big idea, like airbags, and get it done."

The architect of the distracted-driving campaign, U.S. Transportation Secretary Ray LaHood, said his attack on cellphone use while driving has not come at the expense of other safety initiatives. He also has been a vocal advocate for efforts against drunk driving, and for seat-belt use among others. Highway death tolls are at their lowest level since 1950.

Explaining the Data

"This report is completely misleading," LaHood said. "Distracted-driving-related crashes killed nearly 5,500 people in 2009 and injured almost half a million more. Lives are at stake, and all the reputable research we have says that tough laws, good enforcement and increased public awareness will help put a stop to the deadly epidemic of distracted driving on our roads."

The texting issue has been the point of the spear in LaHood's distracted-driving campaign, which has included a pair of major conferences to address the issue. Though he has long advocated that cellphones not be used while driving, sending text messages was deemed more dangerous, and banning the practice was more politically palatable.

Surveys have shown overwhelming support for a ban on text messaging, but the majority of drivers says they want to continue to use their cellphones behind the wheel. That reality played into the debate Sunday [September 26, 2010], when a coalition of state highway safety officials voted against endorsement of a cellphone ban because, as their spokesman put it, "We don't want this to become like the speeding issue, which we've already lost. Everybody speeds."

The institute research found that rather than a decline in texting-related collisions, "there appears to have been a small increase in claims in the states enacting texting bans" which "suggests that texting drivers have responded to the law . . . by hiding their phones from view."

Surveys have shown overwhelming support for a ban on text messaging, but the majority of drivers says they want to continue to use their cellphones behind the wheel.

Lund cautioned that "finding no reduction in crashes, or even a small increase, doesn't mean it's safe to text and drive. . . . It's just that bans aren't reducing this crash risk."

"Our reaction [to the institute report] is that we are not surprised as state enforcement of texting bans is really now just getting underway," said Jonathan Adkins, spokesman for the Governors Highway Safety Association, at whose convention the report was presented. "That said, there is not currently a federal pool of money for states to access for distracted-driving enforcement much like there is for drunk driving and seat-belt use."

In Need of a Sea Change

Lon Anderson, Mid-Atlantic spokesman for AAA [Automobile Association of America], said the institute findings indicated the failure of state legislatures to provide law enforcement with effective laws.

"We have, unfortunately, set the police up for failure," he said. "Would good laws strictly enforced do the job? In our opinion, yes."

Anderson said it will take time for public opinion to get behind the distracted-driving campaign.

"It took a couple of decades before people recognized the problem of drunk driving," he said. "We need to have a sea change on the part of drivers on this issue."

6

Cell Phone Use and Texting Account for Many Traffic Fatalities

Scott Mayerowitz and Lisa Stark

Scott Mayerowitz is a travel and business reporter with ABC News. He has reported on the subprime mortgage industry, unemployment, high gas and oil prices, the travel industry, and the spending habits of the superwealthy. ABC News reporter Lisa Stark specializes in reporting on federal agencies, including the Food and Drug Administration, Federal Aviation Administration, National Transportation Safety Board, the Department of Transportation, and the Transportation Security Administration.

While traffic fatalities have not increased in recent years, many traffic accidents are caused by distracted drivers. Studies show that drivers overestimate their abilities and assume that they can ignore texting bans and other restrictions. This behavior leads to dangerous situations and often results in avoidable crashes.

Think chatting on your cell phone or sending a text message while driving isn't that dangerous? Think again.

So-called distracted driving crashes claimed 5,474 lives and led to 448,000 injuries across the country last year, according to the National Highway Traffic Safety Administration [NHTSA]. That's one in every six highway deaths.

"People [need to] take personal responsibility for the fact that they're driving a three or four thousand pound car,"

Transportation Secretary Ray LaHood told ABC News. "If you're looking down at a cell phone for four seconds or a texting device for four seconds, you're driving the length of a football field without looking at the road."

It Takes Time

Overall traffic fatalities fell in 2009 to their lowest levels since 1950. But as drivers make smarter decisions about wearing seatbelts and not drinking and driving, they are reaching for their cell phones more and more. From 2005 to 2009, the proportion of deaths tied to driver distraction increased to 16 percent from 10 percent, the government said.

"We're right at the starting gate here in terms of where the country was at when nobody buckled up and now 85 percent of the people buckle up," LaHood said. "It took 10 years to get that."

Those under the age of 20 were most likely to be distracted behind the wheel, according to the NHTSA report. However, those ages 30 to 39 were the most likely to be using a cell phone.

"It is very concerning and it's concerning to the extent that most young people think they're invincible," LaHood said. "You need to put the cell phone and the Blackberry in the glove compartment right after you buckle up."

Overall traffic fatalities fell in 2009 to their lowest levels since 1950.

National Distracted Driving Summit

To help raise awareness of the issue, tomorrow [Sept. 21, 2010] LaHood will convene a second National Distracted Driving Summit in Washington that will bring together transportation officials, safety advocates, law enforcement, industry representatives, researchers and family members of victims of distraction-related crashes.

LaHood said that America needs to get tough and start penalizing drivers who text. He said drunk driving deaths didn't go down until the police started arresting people and drivers lost their licenses.

At the same time, there might be a technological solution. LaHood has been speaking with companies about creating a cell phone with a chip in it or a chip in the car that disables the cell phone when the owner is in the driver's seat.

Distracted driving accidents can happen in an instant.

The truck driver, who was texting with his company at the time of the crash, never applied his brakes and hit the cars at 65 mph.

On Jan. 3, 2008, Heather Hurd and her fiancé were on the way to meet with her parents, Russell and Kim Hurd and their wedding planner in Orlando, Fla., when a tractor-trailer driver hit their car—and eight others—while they were stopped at a traffic light.

The truck driver, who was texting with his company at the time of the crash, never applied his brakes and hit the cars at 65 mph.

Heather died at the scene.

"He didn't set out that morning to kill anyone. He was doing his job and part off his job was staying in touch with his company," said Russell Hurd. "He made some poor choices. He was just doing his job, trying to make a living. He's somebody's dad, somebody's grandfather."

In memory of their daughter, the Hurds successfully lobbied for the passage of "Heather's Law" in 2009, which prohibits drivers in their home state of Maryland from texting behind the wheel. They are working to get similar legislation passed in Florida.

"We're really trying to change a culture in the United States. Laws alone don't necessarily stop distracted driving,"

Hurd said. "We're not that naïve to think that just because there's a law that everything's going to stop."

"We want you to turn your cell phone off because we're living proof that in three or four seconds your entire life can change," he added.

Highway Safety, Cell Phones, and Texting

Anne McCartt, senior vice president for research with the Insurance Institute for Highway Safety, said that most drivers probably know that texting or talking on a phone isn't safe.

"So simply reminding them that that's an unsafe thing to do is probably not enough to change their behavior," McCartt said. "When we look at states that have enacted laws limiting phone use, many drivers still persist in talking on phones and texting. Those laws can be very difficult to enforce."

McCartt said most drivers believe that they tend to be safer than other drivers on the road.

"Surveys show that a large majority of drivers think they're better than average drivers so it, people may believe that they can text or talk on a phone safely while other people on the road can't," she said. "With any kind of unsafe driving— drinking and driving, speeding, not wearing your seatbelt— you may get away with that most of the time. You don't think you're going to be in a crash. So it's hard to keep the worry about being in a crash foremost in your mind."

7

Cultural Change Is Needed to Stop Teens from Texting While Driving

Tim Nelson

Tim Nelson is a reporter for Minnesota Public Radio and a 20-year veteran of newspapers across the upper Midwest. He has reported on such topics as education and the Republican National Convention, and he has produced blogs and podcasts.

Despite tougher laws against cell phone use while driving, it will take a change of attitude about risky driving behavior to change teen habits. Education is needed to point out traffic dangers and decrease the allure of "rebellious" behavior on the road that can lead to injury and death.

The deaths of 10 young people in car crashes in Minnesota this spring [2010] may help spur nationwide changes in traffic laws. And it may even change the way Americans drive.

Traffic experts say it takes only about seven seconds to send a text when you're behind the wheel. And that may have been all it took to kill Kelly Phillips.

She was 17 when she died three years ago [in 2007], after a crash near Belle Plaine. Kelly was in the back seat. Her friend was driving and either texting or using an iPod at the same time. They both died.

Kelly's mother, Jane, talked Tuesday [June 1, 2010] about her daughter, one of an estimated 6,000 people a year killed by distracted drivers.

Tim Nelson, "Teens, Traffic Officials Talk About Distracted Driving," Transcript from *Minnesota Public Radio*, June 1, 2010. minnesota.publicradio.org. Copyright © 2010 by Minnesota Public Radio. All rights reserved. Reproduced by permission.

"She was an honors student, a three-sport athlete. Unbelievable kid," said Jane Phillips. "Any parent would love to call her their own, and any student would love to have her as a sister or a best friend. So there is a face behind the statistics. There are people whose lives have been changed forever."

Traffic experts say it takes only about seven seconds to send a text when you're behind the wheel. And that may have been all it took to kill Kelly Phillips.

Changing Teen Behavior

Phillips told her daughter's story to dozens of high school kids, to safe driving advocates and to state and federal officials at a conference at Tartan High School in Oakdale.

They were joined by U.S. Sen. Amy Klobuchar, and National Highway Traffic Safety Administrator David Strickland.

They say this spring's [2010] death toll, including two fatal accidents near Winona and another near Cambridge, underscores the need for tougher regulation of young drivers and a nationwide crackdown on talking and typing behind the wheel.

Klobuchar said she's signed on to federal legislation to ban hand-held cell phones behind the wheel. California, Connecticut and five other states already have such restrictions, but not Minnesota.

Klobuchar also called for a nationwide texting ban and new federal restrictions on young drivers, meant to curtail privileges at first, and only gradually turn them loose on the roads.

"From what I've seen nationally, like 10 to 40 percent decrease in certain accidents when you have that graduated standard, so responsibility is added," she said.

Minnesota already has a texting ban and a graduated driver's license law, which prohibits late-night driving and having too many kids in a car for the first six months a teenager has his or her license.

But Strickland, the federal highway safety administrator, said the standards need to be consistent.

"The goal is to encourage the best and strongest and most effective laws as the foundation for safety. And the only way we can do that is by national legislation," he said.

Strickland said federal seat belt and drunk driving initiatives have already made a difference.

But some lawmakers are skeptical about whether the U.S. is ready to get tougher on teen drivers.

The Culture Must Change

State Rep. Kim Norton, said there has already been pushback in Minnesota regarding restrictions on young drivers. She said some of her legislative colleagues wanted parents to be able to opt out of the program for their kids.

"Minnesota's graduated teen driver's license law is a very mild one. There were many of us that would have preferred it for the full year after you get your license you have these restrictions," Norton said. "Data shows that would have been a far better choice. Other states have that choice. So we did actually loosen up the provisions in the graduated teen license in order to get it passed."

And teens themselves say the law can only go so far.

A fatal crash in April [2010] in southeastern Minnesota was blamed on texting by a teen driver, despite the ban on that practice which went into effect in 2008. Three teens killed near Cambridge recently were on the road in violation of Minnesota's existing graduated licensing law.

"Some kids will say, 'Oh, I'm going to rebel, and I'm going to break this law anyway,'" said Tashie Xiong, head of Tartan High School's chapter of SADD, which has changed its name from Students Against Drunk Driving to Students Against Destructive Decisions—in part a recognition of the other threats to teens, besides drunk driving.

Xiong says in the end, battling distracted driving is going to have to be a cultural change.

"This is a big issue. If I as a student, if I see that it's terrible to text while driving, I think a friend will listen to me, more than a law can tell them," said Xiong.

Congress, though, may weigh in anyway. There are three measures pending on Capitol Hill dealing with cell phones, texting, and new restrictions on young drivers.

8

Use of Navigation Systems Is a Leading Cause of Car Accidents

Mark Macaskill and Kay Smith

Mark Macaskill is a senior reporter at the Sunday Times *(UK). Kay Smith is a journalist, policy researcher and media trainer.*

Even though cellphones have received much of the media attention when it comes to distracted driving, satellite navigation systems are responsible for an alarming number of traffic accidents. Reprogramming the system requires drivers to take their eyes off the road—often too long to avoid obstacles or react to changes in traffic flow. While the electronics industry points to irresponsible drivers violating rules of common sense, the overload of gadgets found in modern cars might entice otherwise capable drivers to lose sight of the traffic.

Sat navs [satellite navigation systems] are the second-most common cause of motoring accidents, according to a new study that suggests thousands of drivers are putting their lives at risk every day by punching routes into the devices while on the move.

In-car satellite navigation systems were implicated in more accidents than mobile phones and were only second to distractions caused by child passengers in a survey of almost 500 UK motorists.

The research, by academics at Heriot-Watt university, has fuelled concern among police and road-safety campaigners because, unlike mobile phones, their use while driving is not explicitly outlawed.

A Standard Feature

Sat navs are now standard, or optional extras, in new cars and sales across Europe doubled last year to almost 14m. It is estimated that a similar number of motorists in Britain own one of the devices.

Punching new information into a sat nav [satellite navigation system] accounted for 2% of accidents, putting them in joint second place with MP3 players.

Terry Lansdown, a senior lecturer of applied psychology at Heriot-Watt and lead author of the new study, analysed the responses of 480 motorists who took part in an online questionnaire to establish the causes of erratic and dangerous driving.

Unruly children were blamed as the most frequent distraction with 2.1% of drivers admitting to an accident.

Punching new information into a sat nav accounted for 2% of accidents, putting them in joint second place with MP3 players. This compares with 1.7% for reading a text message and 1.5% for writing a text message or using a handheld mobile.

A further 1.7% said they had been involved in an accident after following directions on a sat nav. The proportion was the same as those texting on their mobile phone.

Just less than 6% admitted to a "near miss" while entering a new destination into their sat nav or following on-screen advice.

The findings, to be presented this month [September, 2009] at a conference on driver distraction and inattention in

Gothenburg, Sweden, have prompted calls for sat navs to be fitted with a device making it impossible to adjust them unless the car is stationary.

"Following guidance from sat navs reduces the workload of driving but re-setting destinations is very bad practice," said Lansdown.

"Drivers re-setting their sat navs in a simulator at the university demonstrated a difficulty in maintaining their position in a road lane. They weaved around. They also had difficulty maintaining the correct distance from the car in front".

A Much Bigger Problem

Lansdown said the scale of the problem was likely to be far bigger than the findings of his study suggested.

"This is self-reported behaviour so it is likely therefore the problem is even worse than drivers, who may fear identification, are admitting," he said.

Superintendent Alan Duncan, a member of the Scottish road policing officers' committee, which advises the Association of Chief Police Officers in Scotland (Acpos), said the use of sat navs posed a serious threat.

"We would always urge drivers to exercise due care and attention whilst behind the wheel, and to avoid unnecessary distractions.

"A momentary glance at a sat nav is okay but reprogramming it while the vehicle is in motion could be enough to cause a collision. If there's evidence that suggests this is an emerging issue, we will look at it."

A recent survey of more than 2,000 motorists for the insurance company Direct Line suggested as many as 290,000 drivers across the UK had been involved in an accident or near-miss because of their sat nav.

There are concerns the gadgets encourage a variety of dangerous driving behaviours such as dawdling on busy roads, reducing driver awareness and making dangerous, late or illegal turns.

Distractions Are a Serious Problem

In 2008, there were 2,538 fatal road accidents in Britain, including 271 in Scotland.

Drivers need to be trained to pay attention at all times and not to be put off from what can be a developing crash situation just because they are taking a call or dealing with something inside the car.

While there is no explicit ban on adjusting sat navs while driving, the Highway Code warns drivers against in-car distractions. It states: "Do not be distracted by maps or screen-based information, such as navigation or vehicle management systems, while driving or riding. If necessary find a safe place to stop."

However, police have warned that individuals could face a charge of dangerous driving if they have a serious accident while re-programming their sat nav. The offence carries a maximum prison sentence of 14 years and an unlimited fine.

Neil Greig, director of policy and research at the Institute of Advanced Motorists, said: "The main reason for crashing is human error. Drivers need to be trained to pay attention at all times and not to be put off from what can be a developing crash situation just because they are taking a call or dealing with something inside the car."

A spokeswoman for TomTom, one of the leading sat nav manufacturers, said: "Our sat navs are an aid to navigation and we would never suggest people input details whilst driving. [The device] should be kept on the windshield so the driver can keep their eyes on the road."

9

Eating Behind the Wheel
Is a Distraction

Lucia Huntington

Lucia Huntington is a correspondent for the Boston Globe.

Distracted driving is the cause of many of today's traffic acci-dents. In a world of ever-extending commutes and busy sched-ules, eating while operating a vehicle has become the norm, but eating while behind the wheel proves costly for many drivers. Soups, unwieldy burgers, and hot drinks can make steering a car impossible. Although the dangers of eating while driving are ap-parent and well known, drivers ignore them repeatedly, account-ing for many crashes and near-misses.

Carolyn Roesler, 45, of Plainfield, Vt., eats toast in her car while driving to work, even though "there's always a pos-sibility that you'll show up with a few crumbs on your chest."

Northeastern University student Sam Maman, 19, keeps one hand on the wheel while the other holds a slice of pizza. "You can manage it," says the Newton resident. "It's hard to use the phone and the pizza and the car, though."

Helen Cymbala, 54, who lives in Boxford, tells the story of a woman she saw sipping espresso from a tiny china cup while driving in Cambridge. "She had her pinkie finger up in the air," Cymbala says, sounding amazed.

Meals on Wheels

Sound strange? It shouldn't. Studies show that more people eat in their cars, more often, than ever before, according to

Stephen Bailey of Tufts University, an associate professor of anthropology and nutrition—and the food we consider acceptable to eat while we're driving has changed. Once we were a nation on wheels. We're becoming a nation of meals on wheels.

Few of us are strangers to dining and driving, as well as other, more distracting habits on the road. A 2006 study by the National Highway Traffic Safety Administration blamed "inattentive driving" for 80 percent of all car accidents and 65 percent of near-misses. Use of wireless devices accounted for 14.6 percent of the crashes, more than any other cause. Last month the [Barack] Obama administration banned federal and military personnel from texting while driving.

But the study lists other distractions, including daydreaming, personal hygiene, and eating, each of which accounted for 2.1 percent of the total.

"People just get in the car and think, 'I'll do what I have to do,'" says Sergeant James Fitzpatrick of the Lowell Police Department's traffic division.

Drive-Throughs Are Thriving

Not infrequently, that means eating, and for many of us, car fare is the stuff you pull up to a window to order. Seventy percent or more of the Dunkin' Donuts shops in Massachusetts have drive-through windows; 50 to 60 percent of McDonald's sales are made at drive-through windows, according to spokeswomen for the companies.

A 2006 study by the National Highway Traffic Safety Administration blamed "inattentive driving" for 80 percent of all car accidents and 65 percent of near-misses.

Kent Lam of Randolph, 30, likes bagels from Dunkin' Donuts. Joan Jaeger, 58, of North Attleboro, used to go for burgers "because forks and spoons were tricky.

"But once in a while, I would get a Frosty and that you just have to eat with a spoon!" says Jaeger. "Knees come in handy then . . . one hand for the cup, one hand for the spoon, and the knees for the steering wheel."

Fast food isn't the only thing. Jaeger snacks on hard-boiled eggs these days. Cymbala stopped taking along big chunks of meat after she choked on one while driving on the highway; she's made the shift to sandwiches for long trips. And Lynne Molnar, 56, of Cambridge, ate oatmeal with nuts and fruit until a policeman pulled her over for a red-light violation (a judge overturned the ticket) and ordered her and her 11-year-old daughter, Caroline, to throw away their cereal. "That's called littering," Molnar told him pointedly.

Emily Lapkin of Boston, 35, still eats in her Saab—"designed for Euros who would never dream of eating in their cars"—even though when she first started driving she had an accident while eating a quesadilla.

"The only thing worse than quesadillas [are] open-faced bagels with cream cheese," she says. "I once tried this and a hand-over-hand turn resulted in cream cheese all over the steering wheel." Since then, she has switched to supermarket sushi.

Dangerous Appetites

So why not sit down and eat later? Hunger, says Maman, the Northeastern student, who fuels up behind the wheel "usually for lunch or like a pre-dinner dinner."

No time, despite "every day a new chocolate stain on a freshly washed piece of clothing," says a 65-year-old saleswoman who drives six hours a day and wouldn't give her name for fear police might run her license. Last month the knee-steerer navigated through a tire blowout, "hot chocolate between my legs, cookie in my hand."

The need for energy, "some nutrition to make it through the remainder of my day," says Joe Mastroianni, a tile-setter who's in his 40s. "I live on Nantucket, and we don't have fast food. But if I'm on the mainland, I'll stop at Burger King."

Those reasons and more, according to the scientists.

"[Anthropologist] Mary Douglas said a long time ago that food is not feed," says Bailey. But while dining once also meant socializing, "In the last 20 years or so there's been this tendency to make eating simply stuffing your stomach. Basically what happened with fast food and eating in cars is, food has become feed again."

"When we're multitasking, what we're thinking about is how important we must be to have to do all these things all at once . . ."

Food as Feed

Bailey says people are time-starved; he also cites suburbanization and marketing as factors contributing to the trend.

"The popular theory is that we're time-starved; we just don't have enough time in the day," he says. And that carries prestige: "When we're multitasking, what we're thinking about is how important we must be to have to do all these things all at once. . . . [And] the ultimate kind of multitasking is actually feeding yourself while you're doing other stuff."

Suburbanization has meant longer commutes for many workers, and a study of truck drivers by Toyota found that has contributed to a view of the automobile as office and dining room. "People manage their lives out of their trucks, and I think that can be said for most automobiles nowadays," Bailey says.

Then there's marketing, which has widened our expectations about what we can eat in our cars, and made it easier to do so. The standardization of mass-marketed food ("every Big Mac is the same as every other Big Mac," Bailey says) makes it simple to eat more than snacks while we're driving. As Ma-man says, "You really don't need to look at your food while you're eating."

Bailey agrees. "You can eat it without thinking about it. Sandwiches and fries or chips and a drink and maybe a dessert of some kind—it isn't very nutritious, but it is a whole meal."

And it's one that he goes for himself. Asked if he also eats behind the wheel, the professor says, "Oh, God, yes."

"I can dissect this intellectually," he says, "but I get sucked up by it."

10

Some Foods and Drinks Can Lead to Dangerous Distractions

Insure.com

Insure.com provides an array of information on life, health, auto, and home insurance on their website, and offers a library of originally authored insurance articles and decision-making tools.

From coffee to hamburgers, and from pizza to chocolate— American drivers consume any imaginable food behind the wheel. The fast food industry, as well as carmakers, are encouraging the trend by offering more and more foods, cupholders, and cubbies for on-the-go customers. But most foods are messy and dangerous, diverting the driver's attention and leading to otherwise avoidable traffic accidents.

It's tempting if you're in a hurry. It's something that most people have done at one point or another. But eating is a dangerous distraction while you're driving.

The term "distracted driving" refers to anything that takes your eyes, hands or mind away from driving. Eating while driving is one of the most distracting things you can do, according to several surveys by insurance companies and data from the National Highway Traffic Safety Administration (NHTSA). The most recent study, released by NHTSA and the

Virginia Tech Transportation Institute in 2006, reported that 80 percent of all the nation's car crashes involved some type of driver distraction, with "eating on the run" listed as one of the many distractions that plague motorists today.

"Most car accidents are caused by drivers not paying attention," says Eric Bolton, a NHTSA spokesperson.

NHTSA doesn't track specific food-related distractions, but it does track general distractions.

Besides food, common distractions include: outside accidents, adjusting the radio, children, pets, objects moving in the vehicle, drinking beverages, using a cell phone or texting, smoking, putting on makeup, shaving, reading a newspaper, etc.

According to NHTSA, "distraction was most likely to be involved in rear-end collisions in which the lead vehicle was stopped, and in single-vehicle crashes." What makes distraction such a problem is the confluence of the distraction, such as eating, and the unexpected occurrence of events on the road, such as a sharp curve or a driver stopped ahead of you.

Distracting Food

Hagerty Classic Insurance, a provider of classic-car insurance, began to look more closely at this issue after a DMV [Department of Motor Vehicles] check on an insurance applicant turned up a "restraining order" against anything edible within his reach while driving. The man apparently had several previous accidents related to food on his driving record.

Anything that drips is probably not a good idea.

In addition, Hagerty President McKeel Hagerty says his company often receives claims for damage to the interior of classic cars caused by food. "It's tough to replace original wool carpets or particular colors of leather seats," he says.

In looking at the insurer's history of claims, Hagerty found that most drivers had problems in the morning on the way to work, when spills were likely to mar their work attire. That made drivers more anxious to clean up spills while still trying to drive, but didn't necessarily make them more likely to pull off the road to deal with the mess.

Spills Cause Distraction

"It really seems it's more the spill than the eating," says Hagerty. "Anything that drips is probably not a good idea." Hagerty and his staff did a study of their own to see which foods are the worst offenders, and although Hagerty says he ruined a few shirts in the process, they found some interesting information.

Coffee is the top offender because of its tendency to spill. Even in cups with travel lids, somehow the liquid finds its way out of the opening when you drive over a bump, says Hagerty. "I've certainly spilled my share of coffee while I'm driving, and it's not when I'm trying to drink, it's when I hit bumps in the road." And if the stain on your clothes isn't bad enough, the high temperature of most coffees can cause serious burns and distract drivers who are trying to drive while in pain.

The top 10 food offenders in a car are:

1. Coffee: It always finds a way out of the cup.

2. Hot soup: Many people drink it like coffee and run the same risks.

3. Tacos: "A food that can disassemble itself without much help, leaving your car looking like a salad bar," says Hagerty.

4. Chili: The potential for drips and slops down the front of clothing is significant.

5. Hamburgers: From the grease of the burger to ketchup and mustard, it could all end up on your hands, your clothes, and the steering wheel.

6. Barbecued food: The same issue arises for barbecued foods as for hamburgers. The sauce may be great, but if you have to lick your fingers, the sauce will end up on whatever you touch.

7. Fried chicken: Another food that leaves you with greasy hands, which means constantly wiping them on something, even if it's your shirt. It also makes the steering wheel greasy.

8. Jelly or cream-filled donuts: Has anyone eaten a jelly donut without some of the center oozing out? Raspberry jelly can be difficult at best to remove from material.

9. Soft drinks: Not only are they subject to spills, but also the carbonated kind can fizz as you're drinking if you make sudden movements, and most of us remember cola fizz in the nose from childhood. It isn't any more pleasant now.

10. Chocolate: Like greasy foods, chocolate coats the fingers as it melts against the warmth of your skin, and leaves its mark anywhere you touch. As you try to clean it off the steering wheel you're likely to end up swerving.

Most insurance companies don't track specific information on eating and driving. It's too difficult to pin down the exact cause of accidents and separate the various distractions such as cell phone use, talking to passengers, reading the newspaper and eating—all of which drivers engage in while also trying to operate a two-ton piece of machinery.

Manual Transmissions Make Eating-While-Driving Complicated

Hagerty found that driving a car with a stick shift while eating can double the potential for an accident, since one hand is holding food and the other hand is shifting. That leaves no hands for steering, says Hagerty. "When the phone rings, the driving distraction increases significantly and, in a rush to answer, drivers forget they're driving," he says. . . .

The Lawrence Berkeley National Laboratory in California lists 14 items as major causes of driver distraction. Eating and drinking is one of them.

Eating while driving is not only dangerous, it's messy and . . . means you're not watching the road.

"From breakfast burritos to burgers and fries, eating on the run has turned into an everyday part of our lives," its report says. "Eating while driving is not only dangerous, it's messy and . . . means you're not watching the road." The fast food industry allows for eating on the go, with small compact food items that allow for quick consumption. Automobile makers understand the nature of the "on-the-go" lifestyle and have condoned such behavior by making multiple cup holders standard in every vehicle.

The Berkeley Lab offers the following tips for drivers tempted to eat and drive:

Leave a bit early to allow yourself time to stop and eat. If you're traveling with someone, take turns eating and driving.

11

Children in the Backseat Are the Worst Distraction for Drivers

David Petrie

David Petrie's articles on parenthood and education can be found in the Huffington Post.

Noisy kids in the back seat is one driving distraction that has not been addressed by government initiatives that address dangers of distracted driving. Many parents, trying to reign in quarreling siblings or fishing for dropped or thrown items, take their eyes off the road and endanger their families. While the focus on texting-while-driving is laudable, it has failed to address longstanding issues. Yet in both cases—an incoming call and a crying child—drivers should pull over and not attempt to multitask.

Experts at the United States Department of Transportation say there are three types of driver distractions:

- Visual distractions lead drivers to take their eyes off the road.

- Manual distractions lead drivers to take their hands off the wheel.

- Cognitive distractions lead drivers to take their minds off what they're doing.

According to these experts, texting is the most alarming driver activity because it involves all three types of distractions.

Have these experts ever driven in a car with an infant?

Driving with Children Is Dangerous

Driving alone in a car with an infant can be a nightmare. Take my oldest. To keep our house peaceful, we made sure she was completely addicted to Binkies two hours out of the womb. Still, a five-point babyseat harness would send her into such a tizzy that even pacifiers stopped working. When I had to drive her somewhere alone, I'd strap her in to her car seat, then I'd start the car, and then she'd start to wail. I'd give her a pacifier and she'd chuck it onto the floor. I'd drive a quarter mile, stop, retrieve the pacifier, and then repeat the process.

How did I clean the Binky? On good days I had coffee in the car. On bad days . . . I'll save you from the details.

Driving alone in a car with an infant can be a nightmare.

I quickly learned to drive with multiple pacifiers, so as soon as she'd chuck one I'd reach back and pop another one into her mouth. She'd take a few sucks from that pacifier, chuck it, start to scream, and I'd reach back with another one.

While I drove and while my daughter chucked Binkies I dealt with all three types of driver distractions:

- Visual distractions took my eyes off the road as I tried to see where the pacifier landed.

- Manual distractions took my hands off the wheel as I reached behind my seat and fished around the floor.

- Cognitive distractions took my mind off of the road as I asked myself why-oh-why had I ever thought having a child was a good idea.

The Focus on Texting-While-Driving Is Misguided

Distracted driving is a huge problem, but to limit a campaign to one source of distraction is unfortunate at best. One study showed that 60 percent of parents felt driving alone with an infant strapped in a rear-facing car seat in the back seat was "very distracting." Eighty percent feared it could cause an accident. In 2001 the American Automobile Association reported that young children in the car were one of the leading causes of driver-distraction crashes for people ages 20 to 29. Texting might be more widespread now, but the impact of a screaming child certainly hasn't changed.

Distracted driving is a huge problem, but to limit a campaign to one source of distraction is unfortunate at best.

The U.S. Department of Transportation created a website to get people to stop texting while driving. Why haven't they created a website to stop people from driving with kids in the car?

The fix to distracted driving hasn't changed. The Department of Transportation says, "The message is simple—Put it down!" I think they send the wrong message. People are putting their cell phones down—in their laps, so the police can't see them texting behind the wheel. Experts at the Institute for Highway Safety recently said this could increase the risk of accidents.

I think the message needs to be, "Pull over and stop."

When I'd finally lose patience with my daughter I'd pull over and get out. I'd lean against the back of my car, hazard lights flashing, and try to find some inner peace before climbing back behind the wheel. When I pulled over I presented zero risk for crashing. People would stop to ask if I needed help, but once they heard the screaming they'd simply nod and drive away. Out of gas? No problem. That noise? Good luck.

The U.S. Department of Transportation created a website to get people to stop texting while driving. Why haven't they created a website to stop people from driving with kids in the car?

One day my wife discovered a ribbon that came with clips on either end. One clip snapped to the handle of the pacifier and the other end clipped to the car seat. When my daughter chucked the pacifier I only needed to reach back and find the ribbon before reeling in the pacifier like a fish. I felt safer, but the screaming still drove me nuts.

The clip and ribbon weren't perfect. There were times my little girl would chuck her Binky so hard that it would swing around like a tether ball and smack her in the eye. When that happened I suffered from a different driver distraction: laughter.

No Alternatives to Pulling Over

"You don't want that Binky?" I'd snicker to myself. "It looks like that Binky doesn't want you, either."

My kids are all a lot older now, but I still need to pull over at times. Sometimes I do it so quickly that the shock quiets them before we come to a complete stop. I then turn and remind them of two things: I want to drive safely so that they'll live long and healthy lives, and if they don't want to help me drive safely then they can find some other way to get around.

What do you think the message should be? "Put it down," "Pull over and stop," or something else?

12

Multitasking Leads to Distracted Driving

Edmunds.com

Edmunds Inc. publishes three websites seeking to engage and educate automotive consumers, enthusiasts, and insiders.

Multitasking behind the wheel is a potentially deadly habit, but it is probably here to stay. Driven by boredom, arrogance, and ambition, drivers neglect the road and turn to perform tasks such as texting, re-adjusting navigation systems, and eating. Car manufacturers are toeing a thin line between enabling such behavior by installing gadgets, ever-bigger cup holders, and fold-flat seats, and discouraging the same by stopping short of installing food-trays and other conveniences. In a marketplace driven by one-upmanship and electronic gadgets, driver safety often takes a backseat.

Mark Stevens is a multitasking maniac. A couple of months ago [in 2007], the White Plains, New York, marketing consultant was working his cell phone with one hand and his Blackberry with the other while trying to steer his Mercedes SL500 with his wrists and knees—when he plowed it into a rental vehicle in an Enterprise parking lot. That followed his fourth ticket in four years for talking on his cell phone while driving.

"If you are a determined multitasker, it's an addiction—and you can't stop it," said the 59-year-old Stevens.

Talk about distracted driving. Even during a short trek, he said, he's likely to sip a Diet Coke and a bottled water, eat a sandwich, read a copy of *The Economist*, write notes to himself and listen to NPR [National Public Radio], in addition to performing his cell phone and Blackberry action—oh, *and* driving. "I'm a driven person, and that's why I do all this stuff while I drive." Efficiency, not safe driving, is primary.

The Power of Arrogance and Ambition

Although he may represent an extreme, there's a little bit of Stevens in many of us. Multitasking while driving has become endemic—and epidemic—on American roads. More drivers are trying to figure out what other duties they can perform while driving. Insurance companies, meanwhile, are trying to make drivers keep their eyes on the road and their hands on the wheel. And automakers are caught between consumer demands for more capabilities and conveniences—and the safety and legal concerns that often compel vehicle designers to make multitasking more difficult.

If you are a determined multitasker, it's an addiction— and you can't stop it.

The growing number of cultural references to multitasking resonates with all of us. They include the TV ad depicting a group of business colleagues moving all their office functions into a car and the Allstate Insurance commercial in which spokesman Dennis Haysbert *tsk-tsks* viewers about multitasking.

The reasons for multitasking are many. Ever-longer commutes are tempting time-starved Americans to invent ways to spread more tasks over the hours they must spend in their vehicles. Also blame cell phones, video entertainment systems and iPods. Throw in the fact that many drivers apparently don't care that they might be annoying—or even alarming—

other drivers by applying mascara, drinking hot coffee, reading a pulp novel or selecting station XM 132 all at the same time.

A recent survey by Nationwide Insurance quantified some of the trend's scary dimensions. More than 80 percent of drivers surveyed identified themselves as multitaskers. Sixty-eight percent eat while driving; texting or instant-messaging while driving, or fixing hair, is practiced by 19 percent of drivers; 14 percent comfort or discipline children while behind the wheel; and 8 percent drive with a pet in their laps.

Driving in Near-Oblivion

Weather conditions had little effect on drivers' tendency to multitask. Even those who perceive themselves as safe drivers admitted doing outlandish things behind the wheel, including changing clothes, balancing a checkbook and shaving.

> *Ever-longer commutes are tempting time-starved Americans to invent ways to spread more tasks over the hours they must spend in their vehicles.*

And multitasking is going to increase before it wanes. About 35 percent of Gen Y-ers say they always multitask, compared with 30 percent of Gen X-ers and just 21 percent of baby boomers. Those differences are amplified in important behaviors such as fiddling with a cell phone while driving: 37 percent of Gen Y-ers admit doing it versus just 17 percent of Gen X-ers and only 2 percent of boomers. About 89 percent of teenagers reported seeing other teens on their cell phones at least sometimes while driving, reports a recent State Farm Insurance survey.

The problem for drivers and insurance companies is that drivers are just bad at multitasking successfully. About 80 percent of all crashes are related to some form of distracted driving, according to the U.S. government.

"Driver behavior is only getting worse," said Bill Windsor, associate vice president of safety for Columbus-based Nationwide Insurance. "Car design and safety features have helped reduce fatalities over the last 10 years, but there are signs—such as an increase in fatalities among pedestrians and motorcyclists—that problems with driving behavior are starting to outstrip vehicle and roadway improvements."

Governments, insurance companies and other players can mitigate the problem to some extent. Four states and the District of Columbia already outlaw the use of handheld phones while driving, and at least 38 states currently are debating bills that would specifically regulate text messaging while behind the wheel, according to the National Conference of State Legislatures. Highway designers are trying to add more rumble strips on highway shoulders to startle those who've strayed to the side, and creating greater numbers of safe rest spots along the nation's roads.

The problem for drivers and insurance companies is that drivers are just bad at multitasking successfully. About 80 percent of all crashes are related to some form of distracted driving, according to the U.S. government.

Automakers Need to Intervene

But a large part of the responsibility and opportunity for dealing with multitasking rests with automakers themselves. The scope of their dilemma is perfectly underscored by the fact that an alliance of General Motors, Toyota, Nissan and Ford spent $6 million over the last four years to study driver distraction and develop solutions. Their conclusion was that drivers can safely withstand just about any amount of aural distraction in a vehicle as long as they keep their vision on the road in front of them.

"It was a lot of expensive research just to validate the idea that you should keep your eyes on the road," admits Rich Deering, GM's senior manager of crash-avoidance system development. "But this is an issue that won't go away."

The auto industry is pulled in two directions. As quality and other differences among vehicle brands have dwindled over the last generation, car companies have turned to comfort and convenience features in their battle for market share. In the process, they have converted many of their vehicles into rolling living rooms and offices. Passengers are invited to watch movies, thanks to rear-seat entertainment systems; work on their laptops, courtesy of ample power outlets (including 110 volt connections) throughout the vehicle; and use OnStar to tap into sports scores and stock-price quotes on the Internet.

Vehicle designers even encourage drivers to engage in more multitasking by, for example, increasing the capabilities of audio systems, providing devices and slots to facilitate mobile-phone usage, and cramming every square inch around the driver with drink holders, trays and even laptop compartments.

It's hard to keep drivers away from all those distracting goodies that, nominally at least, are meant only for passengers to enjoy.

"We need to provide reasonable accommodations for a wide variety of activities that people want to do in their cars," said Andrew Coetzee, vice president of product planning for Toyota Motor Sales, USA. "We do have responsibilities to meet the needs of customers. It's up to customers to use them at their discretion."

Yet automakers have taken measures to limit multitasking by drivers—or at least make it safer—in specific areas:

Navigation Systems and Bluetooth

The industry's unspoken agreement bans navigation screens that require drivers to lower their heads more than 30 degrees from a straight-ahead position. Also, many automakers won't allow front-seat occupants to enter destination addresses manually while the vehicle is in motion.

Despite some states' laws to the contrary, drivers aren't going to stop using cell phones while driving.

Meanwhile, they're all working on improving voice-recognition technology so drivers won't have to touch navigation screens at all. Based on several years of experience with its OnStar system—which relies on a customer-service person to give drivers oral directions—GM is convinced that voice interaction largely takes the danger out of navigation systems. "We're just not seeing a crash problem there because, with OnStar, drivers can keep their eyes on the road," Deering said.

Despite some states' laws to the contrary, drivers aren't going to stop using cell phones while driving. So automakers are doing their best to make it as safe as possible. Installing hands-free technologies such as Bluetooth across their entire lineups is a major focus. "There's a social responsibility we feel in developing a system like that," said Coetzee. "It's taking a more reasonable approach than just saying, 'Don't use a cell phone when you drive.'"

Automakers are pushing to integrate vehicle sound systems on digital platforms and to create easy interfaces with MP3 players so there is a central, convenient source of control on the dash—instead of the makeshift assemblages of iPod cradles, extenders, power-port plug-ins and other devices that many drivers now use. Most vehicles already are available with steering-wheel-mounted audio controls.

Making Multitasking Safer

Many vehicles now offer fold-down front passenger seats with flat backs that drivers can use as makeshift desks, as well as 110-volt power ports to power their laptops.

[Food and beverage handling] ... is an area that exemplifies how automakers can enhance the multitasking experience without making it more distracting or dangerous—the ultimate win-win tactic. Chrysler, for example, figures that as long as you're going to demand drink holders, they might as well help you maintain the beverage temperature you want. So in the Chrysler Sebring and Dodge Avenger sedans, there's a cupholder option that allows drivers to keep drinks warm or cool. Other manufacturers have expanded the number, sizes and locations of their front-seat cupholders to put beverages within easier reach. Even the tiny Mazda Miata now has door-mounted cupholders capable of holding a regular size Starbucks coffee.

Chrysler, for one, has drawn the line at installing food trays up front. "We actually looked at a compartment that would hold a fast-food hamburger or other sandwich," said Ralph Gilles, a product vice president for Chrysler's Jeep unit. "But that was the point where we were inviting a little more activity than we really want from the driver. And what could you add for food beyond that?"

Because there's no sign whatsoever that Americans are going to multitask less, auto designers are going to have more and more such internal discussions—leading to increasingly difficult decisions.

"You could say we're only helping the dysfunctionality of America with some of the things we do in vehicles now," Gilles said. "But it's the reality of the marketplace."

Organizations to Contact

The editors have compiled the following list of organizations concerned with the issues debated in this book. The descriptions are derived from materials provided by the organizations. All have publications or information available for interested readers. The list was compiled on the date of publication of the present volume; names, addresses, phone and fax numbers, and e-mail and Internet addresses may change. Be aware that many organizations take several weeks or longer to respond to inquiries, so allow as much time as possible.

AAA Foundation for Traffic Safety
607 14th Street NW, Suite 201, Washington, DC   20005
(202) 638-5944 • fax: (202) 638-5943
website: www.aaafoundation.org

The AAA Foundation for Traffic Safety is dedicated to saving lives and reducing injuries by preventing traffic accidents. It is a not-for-profit, publicly supported charitable educational and research organization and provides newsletters and annual reports on its website.

The Alliance of Automobile Manufacturers
1401 Eye Street, NW, Suite 900, Washington, DC   20005
(202) 326-5500 • fax: (202) 326-5598
website: www.autoalliance.org

The Alliance of Automobile Manufacturers supports a ban on text messaging or making phone calls using a handheld device while driving. The Alliance supports an approach that addresses the issue while preserving opportunities to enhance safety. It publishes its articles on drivers' safety online.

American Driver & Traffic Safety Association
Highway Safety Services, LLC, Indiana, PA   15701
(724) 801-8246 • fax: (724) 349-5042
website: www.adtsea.org

The American Driver and Traffic Safety Education Association (ADTSEA) is the professional association representing traffic safety educators throughout the United States and abroad. Research articles on distracted driving and other traffic safety concerns can be accessed on their website.

National Highway Traffic Safety Administration (NHTSA)
1200 New Jersey Avenue, SE, Washington, DC   20590
(888) 327-4236
website: www.nhtsa.org

The National Highway Traffic Safety Administration (NHTSA), under the US Department of Transportation, was established by the Highway Safety Act of 1970. The agency is committed to achieving the highest standards of excellence in motor vehicle and highway safety, and works to help prevent crashes and their attendant costs, both human and financial. Reports and articles are published online and available on their website.

Federal Communications Commission (FCC)
445 12th Street SW, Washington, DC   20554
(888) 225-5322 • fax: (866) 418-0232
e-mail: fccinfo@fcc.gov
website: www.fcc.gov

The Federal Communications Commission (FCC) is an independent United States government agency. It was established by the Communications Act of 1934 and regulates interstate and international communications by radio, television, wire, satellite, and cable. The FCC's jurisdiction covers the 50 states, the District of Columbia, and US possessions. Articles and reports on distracted driving are available online.

FocusDriven
P.O. Box 2262, Grapevine, TX   76099
(630)775-2405
e-mail: info@focusdriven.org
website: www.focusdriven.org

FocusDriven supports victims of cell phone distracted driving and families of victims. It is dedicated to increasing public awareness of the dangers of distracted driving and promoting corresponding public policies, programs, and personal responsibility.

The Insurance Institute for Highway Safety

1005 N. Glebe Road, Suite 800, Arlington, VA   22201
(703) 247-1500 • fax: 703/247-1588
website: www.iihs.org

The Insurance Institute for Highway Safety (IIHS) is a nonprofit research and communications organization funded by auto insurers. The IIHS tests and investigates measures seeking to prevent motor vehicle accidents and works to reduce injuries in the accidents that do occur. It publishes the traffic newsletter *Status Report.*

National Highway Traffic Safety Administration (NHTSA)

1200 New Jersey Avenue, SE, Washington, DC   20590
(888) 327-4236
website: http://www.nhtsa.gov

The National Highway Traffic Safety Administration (NHTSA) has developed a three tier approach to helping teen drivers become safer behind the wheel. These three tiers include parents talking to their kids about driver safety; spelling out the rules; and setting behavior standards. Articles and reports such as "Factors Related to Fatal Single-Vehicle Run-Off-Road Crashes" can be accessed on the NHTSA website.

National Safety Council (NSC)

1121 Spring Lake Dr., Itasca, IL   60143-3201
(630) 285-1121 • fax: (630) 285-1315
e-mail: info@nsc.org
website: www.nsc.org

The National Safety Council (NSC) is dedicated to saving lives by preventing injuries and deaths at work, in homes and communities, and on the roads. The NSC partners with businesses, elected officials, and the public to make an impact in areas such as distracted driving, teen driving, workplace safety, and safety in the home and community. Their website provides information to both parents and teenagers about modifying risky behavior while driving.

Network of Employers for Traffic Safety (NETS)
344 Maple Avenue, West, # 357, Vienna, VA   22180-56122
703-273-6005
e-mail: nets@trafficsafety.org.
website: www.trafficsafety.org

The Network of Employers for Traffic Safety (NETS) is an employer-led public/private partnership seeking to improve the safety and health of employees and their families. NETS is committed to preventing traffic crashes that occur both on- and off-the-job. NETS publishes a monthly electronic newsletter and makes articles on cell phone safety available online.

US Department of Transportation (DOT)
1200 New Jersey Ave, SE, Washington, DC   20590
(202) 366-4000
website: www.dot.gov

The Department of Transportation (DOT) works to ensure a fast, safe, efficient, accessible, and convenient transportation system that meets vital national interests. Detailed resources can be accessed at DOT's website www.distraction.gov, and statistics on traffic accidents can be found at The Bureau of Transportation Statistics' website, at www.bts.gov.

Virginia Tech Transportation Institute (VTTI)
3500 Transportation Research Plaza, Blacksburg, VA   24061
(540) 231-1500 • fax: (540) 231-1555
e-mail: info@vtti.vt.edu
website: www.vtti.vt.edu

The Virginia Tech Transportation Institute (VTTI) is Virginia Tech's largest research center and seeks to save lives, save time, and save money in the transportation field by developing and using state-of-the-art tools, techniques, and technologies. Its research is effecting significant change in public policies in the transportation domain on both the state and national levels. Reports, such as *The Impact of Driver Inattention on Near-Crash/Crash Risk*, are published online.

Bibliography

Books

Tomi Ahonen   *Mobile as 7th of the Mass Media: Cellphone, Cameraphone, iPhone, Smartphone*. London: futuretext, 2008.

Naomi Baron   *Always On: Language in an Online and Mobile World*. New York: Oxford University Press, 2010.

Susan Brenner   *Law in an Era of Smart Technology*. New York: Oxford University Press, 2007.

David Crystal   *Txtng: The Gr8 Db8*. New York: Oxford University Press, 2008.

Shawn Marie Edgington   *Read Between the Lines: A Humorous Guide to Texting with Simplicity and Style*. Dallas, TX: Brown Publishing Group, 2009.

Charles Ess   *Digital Media Ethics: Digital Media and Society*. Cambridge, England: Polity, 2009.

Gerard Goggin   *Global Mobile Media*. London: Routledge, 2010.

Gerard Goggin   *Cell Phone Culture: Mobile Technology in Everyday Life*. London: Routledge, 2006.

Gerard Goggin and Larissa Hjorth — *Mobile Technologies: From Telecommunications to Media.* London: Routledge, 2009.

Margaret Johnson — *Drive Right: You Are the Driver.* Old Tappan, NJ: Prentice Hall, 2007.

Kolby McHale — *Why Cell Phones and Driving Don't Mix and the Laws on Using Cell Phones While Driving Including Texting.* Webster's Digital Services, 2011.

Michael Regan — *Driver Distraction: Theory, Effects, and Mitigation.* New York: Taylor & Francis, 2008.

United States Congress House of Representatives — *Addressing the Problem of Distracted Driving.* BiblioGov, 2010.

Steven Vedro — *Digital Dharma: A User's Guide to Expanding Consciousness in the Infosphere.* Wheaton, IL: Quest Books, 2007.

Tony Wilson — *Understanding Media Users: From Theory to Practice.* West Sussex, United Kingdom: Wiley-Blackwell, 2008.

Kristie Young, John Lee, and Michael Regan, editors — *Driver Distraction: Theory, Effects, and Mitigation.* Boca Raton, FL: CRC Press, 2008.

Periodicals and Internet Sources

Michael Austin	"Texting While Driving: How Dangerous Is it?" *Car and Driver Magazine*, June 2009.
Kristen Beede and Steven Kass	"Engrossed in Conversation: The Impact of Cell Phones on Simulated Driving Performance," *Accident Analysis & Prevention*, March 2006.
Myra Blanco, Wayne Blevera, John Gallaghera, and Thomas Dingus	"The Impact of Secondary Task Cognitive Processing Demand on Driving Performance," *Accident Analysis & Prevention*, September 2006.
Sherri Box	"New Data from Virginia Tech Transportation Institute Provides Insight into Cell Phone Use and Driving Distraction," *Virginia Tech News*, July 29, 2009.
Terry Bunn et al.	"Sleepiness/Fatigue and Distraction/Inattention as Factors for Fatal Versus Nonfatal Commercial Motor Vehicle Driver Injuries," *Accident Analysis & Prevention*, September 2005.
Larry Copeland	"Driver Phone Bans' Impact Doubted," *USA Today*, January 29, 2010.
Larry Copeland	"States Go After Texting Drivers," *USA Today*, January 24, 2010.

The Council of State Governments	"Restricting Use of Mobile Devices in Cars," *Trends in America*, September 2009.
Daily Herald	"GPS Products Must Adapt to Beat out Cell Phone Apps," *Daily Herald (Arlington Heights, IL)*, November 29, 2009.
Daily Herald	"Still Talking When Driving, despite the Law," *Daily Herald (Arlington Heights, IL)*, June 10, 2008.
Birsen Donmez, Linda Ng Boyle, and John D. Lee	"Safety Implications of Providing Real-Time Feedback to Distracted Drivers," *Accident Analysis & Prevention*, May 2007.
Birsen Donmez, Linda Ng Boyle, and John D. Lee	"The Impact of Distraction Mitigation Strategies on Driving Performance," *Human Factors: The Journal of the Human Factors and Ergonomics Society*, 2006.
David Eby, Lidia Kostyniuk, and Jonathan Vivoda	"Risky Driving: Relationship Between Cellular Phone and Safety Belt Use," *Transportation Research Record: Journal of the Transportation Research Board*, 2003.
David Eby, Jonathan Vivoda, and Renée St. Louis	"Driver Hand-held Cellular Phone Use: A Four-year Analysis," *Journal of Safety Research*, vol. 37, no. 3, 2006.
The Federal Communications Commission	"Distracted Driving," June 4, 2010.

Nancy Gibbs — "Cell-Phone Second Thoughts," *Time*, March, 5, 2009.

Gerard Goggin — "Adapting the Mobile Phone: The iPhone and its Consumption." *Continuum: Journal of Media & Cultural Studies*, April 2009.

Stephanie Hanes — "Texting While Driving: The New Drunk Driving," *Christian Science Monitor*, November 5, 2009.

Richard Hanowski et al. — "The Drowsy Driver Warning System Field Operational Test: Data Collection Methods," *National Highway Traffic Safety Administration*, 2008.

Katherine E. Heck and Ramona M. Carlos — "Passenger Distractions Among Adolescent Drivers," *Journal of Safety Research*, vol. 39, no. 4, 2008.

William J. Horrey and Mary F. Lesch — "Driver-initiated Distractions: Examining Strategic Adaptation for In-vehicle Task Initiation," *Accident Analysis & Prevention*, January 2009.

Murray Iain — "Cell Phone Accidents," *American Enterprise*, January 2005.

Yoko Ishigami and Raymond M. Klein — "Is a Hands-free Phone Safer than a Handheld Phone?" *Journal of Safety Research*, vol. 40, no. 2, 2009.

Melissa Jenco	"Too Young to Drive—and Use the Phone? Legislation Would Ban Cell Phone Use Among Those with Learners Permits," *Daily Herald (Arlington Heights, IL)*, February 5, 2005.
Anne T. McCartt	"Driven to Distraction: Technological Devices and Vehicle Safety," *Insurance Institute for Highway Safety*, November 4, 2009.
Jeffrey Muttart, Donald Fisher, Mike Knodler, and Alexande Pollatsek	"Driving Without a Clue: Evaluation of Driver Simulator Performance During Hands-free Cell Phone Operation in a Work Zone," *Transportation Research Record: Journal of the Transportation Research Board*, 2007.
Jack Nasar, Peter Hecht, and Richard Wener Richard	"Mobile Telephones, Distracted Attention, and Pedestrian Safety," *Accident Analysis and Prevention*, January 2008.
National Conference of State Legislatures, Budgets and Revenue Committee	"Special Edition: Transportation," *Mandate Monitor*, November 5, 2009.
New York Times	"Gauging Your Distraction," July 19, 2009.

Michael Rakauskasa, et al.	"Combined Effects of Alcohol and Distraction on Driving Performance," *Accident Analysis and Prevention*, 2008.
Register-Guard (Eugene, OR)	"Cell Phone Quandaries," April 23, 2009.
Sandy Smith	"Danger Ahead! Cell Phones and Driving," *Occupational Hazards*, July 2008.
David L. Strayer et al.	"A Comparison of the Cell-phone Driver and the Drunk Driver," *Human Factors: The Journal of the Human Factors and Ergonomics Society*, Summer 2006.
David L. Strayer and Frank A. Drews	"Profiles in Driver Distraction: Effects of Cell Phone Conversations on Younger and Older Drivers," *Human Factors: The Journal of the Human Factors and Ergonomics Society*, Winter 2004.
THE Journal	"Sending the Right Message," May 1, 2009.
US National Highway Traffic Safety Administration	"State Laws on Distracted Driving," January 26, 2010.
Washington Times	"Cell Phone Controls Alarm System," August 12, 2009

Washington Times "Distraction Destruction; Dialing Cell Phone, Doing Makeup Top Crash-Defying Driving Habits," June 22, 2006.

Index